INSPIRATIONAL LIVES

STEVE JOBS
DIGITAL INNOVATOR

Adam Sutherland

WAYLAND

Daring to be different

Steve Jobs was a man who liked to think differently. As the founder of Apple computers, he took on the dominance of the PC manufacturers and their boring grey boxes – and won. **Obsessed** with the idea of blending technology with great design, Steve brought the world the iMac, the iPod, the iPhone and the iPad, creating some of the most memorable products of the 20th and 21st centuries and bringing fun to an industry that was previously only interested in function.

HONOURS BOARD

Steve's greatest hits

1977 *The Apple II computer: sold 5-6 million*

1998 *The iMac: sold 20 million*

2001 *The iPod: sold 320 million (to December 2011)*

2007 *The iPhone: sold 183 million (to April 2012)*

2010 *The iPad: sold 70 million (to April 2012)*

Under Steve's leadership, Apple became the wealthiest and most successful company on the planet, and Steve himself was a millionaire many times over. But unlike most businessmen, Steve was well-known – even loved – by the people who bought Apple's products.

Steve Jobs at the launch of the iPhone in 2007.

When Steve died from pancreatic cancer on 5 October 2011, millions of people around the world turned out to **mourn**. Crowds gathered outside Apple stores from Santa Monica to Beijing, building makeshift shrines, lighting candles in remembrance and leaving half-eaten apples in homage to the firm's iconic logo.

Such a massive outpouring of affection for a businessman was unique. Steve was just 56 when he died, but his lasting **legacy** was to touch people's lives and even improve them through technology. As the *Los Angeles Times* wrote, '[Steve was] the face of the personal technology revolution... an era when people brought computers into their homes, when portable phones and music players [appeared in] every pocket, and when excitement about electronic devices crossed over... to the mainstream.'

This book follows Steve's story. Where he was born, where he went to school, what drove him to success. Read on for the real story of the man behind Apple.

WOW!

When Steve Jobs died, Apple had $76 billion (£47bn) in the bank – equal to the combined stock market values of Sainsbury's, Marks and Spencer, Barclays and Burberry!

A memorial to Steve outside the Apple store on Regent Street, London. Similar displays of affection were seen around the world after Steve's death in 2011.

You will be missed Steve
-Austin, USA

The orphan who found a family

Steve was born in San Francisco in 1955, and put up for adoption by his birth mother, a young unmarried student. The baby was soon adopted by a local couple and named Steven Paul Jobs.

Steve's adoptive father, Paul, was an ex-US Navy Coast Guard who held a range of jobs, from estate agent to engineer. By the time Steve was ten, the family had moved to Mountain View, California, a community close to San Francisco in the heart of an area that became known as Silicon Valley.

Mountain View was home to a growing number of electronics companies, including the country's largest, Hewlett-Packard, and every weekend Steve would see his new neighbours tinkering with inventions in their garages and workshops.

The Jobs' family home in Los Altos, California. Steve founded Apple in the garage in 1976.

INSPIRATION

When Steve was six years old, his father gave him some tools and a small workbench and showed him how to build things. He also taught Steve the basics of electronics, which sparked a life-long interest in technology.

Steve was an extremely bright student, but was often in trouble at school. He enjoyed dreaming up ways to disrupt lessons or play tricks on his teachers rather than learning! Fortunately, Steve's life in Mountain View gave him an interest in electronics.

In 1969, he met Steve Wozniak, a fellow technology fan. Woz, as he was known, was a few years older than Steve, and had a reputation as the local electronics whizz-kid. 'He was the first person I met who knew more about electronics than I did,' Steve remembered.

Steve (right) and Apple co-founder Steve Wozniak (left). Wozniak was the programming genius, while Steve had the ambition to change the world!

After high school, Steve persuaded his parents to send him to the expensive Reed College in Oregon. While he was there, he became fascinated with Eastern belief systems and ideas, and experimented with all-fruit diets, and a routine of going without washing for weeks, in the belief that his body would start to self-clean!

Steve quickly got bored with the academic **syllabus** at Reed, and left college without graduating, returning to Silicon Valley to find work. The story goes that one day he turned up at the reception desk of games manufacturer Atari looking scruffy and unwashed saying he wouldn't leave until they gave him a job! The plan worked, and Steve was duly employed as a junior programmer.

WOW!

While he was at Atari, Steve was offered a bonus of $1,000 (£618) to create the game Break-Out (like Brickbreaker). He got Woz to design it, gave Woz $300 (£185) and kept the rest!

The founding of Apple

Steve and Woz had very different personalities – Steve the fast-talking **extrovert**, Woz the typical **introverted** computer programmer – but they bonded over a shared love of technology.

After he finished college, Woz found a job at Hewlett-Packard, and Steve would often ask for Woz's help on various programming problems he was facing at Atari. Together the pair threw themselves into California's new hi-tech scene, which grew around a group of computer enthusiasts (known as 'hobbyists') called the Homebrew Computer Club. Woz had the programming expertise, but it was Steve who had the drive to turn their hobby into a business that would change the world.

When the world's first personal computer appeared in 1975, Steve started planning how he could make money in this new area. With Woz he formed Apple Computer – named after his love of music (The Beatles' record label was also called Apple), and – always competitive – because it would come before Atari in the phone book!

The original multicoloured Apple logo, seen here at the entrance to Apple headquarters in Cupertino, California in 2000.

WOW!

Steve commissioned graphic designer Rob Janoff to create the original Apple Rainbow logo in 1976. There's a bite taken out of it so people didn't think it was a tomato!

Woz started building circuit boards that hobbyists could then load up with **components** to create their own basic 'computer'.

The plan was to build the boards for $25 each (£15), and sell them for $50 (£30). Instead, Steve persuaded local computer store owner Paul Terrell to sell ready-stocked boards. These boards, launched in 1976, were called Apple Is. Terrell's shop ordered 50 at $500 each (£310) – a first order worth $25,000 (£15.500)!

The following year, with Woz still working full time at Hewlett-Packard, the pair launched the Apple II. Coming with its own built-in monitor, keyboard and sound, it was the world's first complete computer, and the first one designed for the mass market, not just engineers and computer 'nerds'. Steve believed that 'computers are for everyone' and aimed Apple at the home market and not just technology experts – an idea the company still uses today.

INSPIRATION

'Steve Jobs didn't... set the direction of my Apple I and Apple II designs but he did the more important part of turning them into a product that would change the world.' **Steve Wozniak**

The young members of a San Francisco computer club try out the new Apple IIC in 1984.

Steve leaves Apple

The success of the Apple II helped the company to grow fast. By 1980, Apple employed over 1,000 people in the US and overseas. Steve and his fellow directors started making plans to 'go public', meaning they would offer Apple shares for sale on the stock exchange in New York.

In December 1980, 4.6 million Apple shares went on sale, and were bought within an hour. Overnight Steve's share of the company was worth $217.5m (£134.5m)! He was not only one of the richest men in America, but as the handsome, intelligent founder of one of the country's most admired technology companies, he was often seen on TV and on the covers of magazines, and was an inspiration to millions of young **entrepreneurs**.

Steve (pictured right) entertains Apple president John Sculley at a conference in Phoenix, Arizona in 1984.

WOW!

Steve persuaded Pepsi president John Sculley to join Apple by asking him the question, 'Are you going to sell sugar water for the rest of your life when you could be doing something really important?'

Steve's wealth didn't stop him working as hard as ever. However, as a boss he was often difficult to please. He set very high standards for himself and for his employees, and he would often shout and scream, and even reduce people to tears if he didn't think their work was good enough. On the flipside, everyone at Apple knew that working with Steve could also be an exciting and eye-opening process, and there was always competition among employees to be on his team, despite the 80-hour-per-week workload that Steve demanded!

As the company's founder, Steve was able to pursue projects that interested him, without asking anyone else's permission. He put a lot of Apple's time and money into new machines like the Apple III and the Lisa (named after his first child, Lisa Brennan-Jobs, born in 1978) and unfortunately both machines flopped.

Now Steve was running a 'public' company, he had a responsibility to the shareholders who had invested in Apple. By 1985, the company's shares had started to fall on the stock market. The board decided to remove Steve as chairman and put someone else in charge. Steve resigned and sold all but one of his shares.

INSPIRATION

In 1984 Steve spent over $1 million (£618,000) on a TV ad to launch the Macintosh computer. The ad, which ran during the Superbowl (the US equivalent to the FA Cup Final) was directed by Ridley Scott, who made *Aliens* and *Blade Runner*.

Steve (pictured left) and John Sculley present the new Macintosh desktop computer at an Apple shareholder meeting in Cupertino, California in 1984.

To infinity and beyond

Although Steve was a multi-millionaire, he still loved to work and was keen to get back into the technology business. He quickly started to look around for new opportunities.

The same year that Steve left Apple, he launched a new company, NeXT, with the aim of producing high-end business computers. He also bought a small animation studio from *Star Wars* director George Lucas called Industrial Light & Magic. The company specialised in set building, model making and traditional special effects, but it had a team in place (led by ex-Disney animator John Lasseter) that was working on computer animation. Steve renamed the company Pixar.

Steve quickly realised that he now owned not only the most sophisticated computer animation systems in the country, but also that he employed some of the world's most talented animators! Nevertheless, Pixar was far from an instant success, and at one stage was losing nearly $1 million (£600.000) every month. Steve had to fund the company's losses himself, and came close to shutting the company down several times.

The Pixar team, including Steve (far left) and creative head John Lasseter (second from right) gather for a screening of Finding Nemo *in 2003.*

WOW!

Steve bought Pixar for $10m (£6.1m) in 1986 and sold it to Disney in 2006 for $7.4bn (£4.5bn)!

Pixar's major breakthrough was a short piece called *Tin Toy*, created by Lasseter and his team, which won the first ever Oscar for computer animation. This award caught the interest of animation giant Disney, who wanted to discuss the idea of a partnership between the two companies.

Steve was a great **negotiator**, and when he met Disney bosses, he gave them no indication of the financial trouble that Pixar was in. Instead, he made the world-famous film company feel they were lucky to be dealing with Pixar at all! Disney agreed to fund, **promote** and distribute three Pixar movies, starting with *Toy Story* in 1995. The story of Buzz and Woody made over $350 million (£215m) around the world and was nominated for three Oscars. Steve was back on top.

HONOURS BOARD
Pixar's greatest hits
1995 *Toy Story*
1998 *A Bug's Life*
1999 *Toy Story 2*
2001 *Monsters, Inc*
2003 *Finding Nemo*
2004 *The Incredibles*
2006 *Cars*
2007 *Ratatouille*
2008 *WALL-E*
2009 *Up*
2010 *Toy Story 3*

To date, Pixar has won 26 Oscars, seven Golden Globes and three Grammys. Its films have made over $6.3 billion (£3.9bn) worldwide.

Finding Nemo, *the story of a clownfish's ocean-wide search for his son, broke box office records when it was released in 2003, and won an Oscar for Best Animated Film.*

A change of life

For many years, Steve put his work life before his personal life. However, while he was struggling to build two new businesses from scratch, he also met the woman who would soon become his wife.

In October 1989, Steve accepted an invitation to speak at Stanford Business School. Laurene Powell, a post-graduate student, attended the lecture and sat next to Steve in the front row while he was waiting to go on stage. The pair got chatting, and Steve asked Laurene out to dinner that night. As he later joked, 'We walked into town and we've been together ever since.'

The happy couple: Steve and wife Laurene Powell attending a Pixar exhibition at the New York Museum of Modern Art in 2005.

WOW!

Steve became known for his simple work outfit – a black long-sleeved turtleneck, Levi's 501 jeans and New Balance trainers. He told friends he liked the simplicity of wearing the same outfit every day.

Steve and Laurene were married in Yosemite National Park in 1991. Their son Reed was born at the end of the year, daughter Erin followed in 1995, and youngest daughter Eve in 1998.

Marriage and parenthood might have given Steve's life some much-needed balance, but they certainly didn't slow down his business instincts. In 1996, a new Apple chairman, Gil Amelio, was announced. Steve called him to offer his support. He still cared deeply for his old company, and Steve explained to Gil that as the company's co-founder he was the only man to put Apple back on track.

Gil took Steve's job application surprisingly well. At the time, Apple was searching for a new operating system for their next wave of computers, and decided to buy Steve's company NeXT in order to incorporate their technology into new Apple machines.

Steve was finally back at Apple, but even with a new NeXT operating system, the company's fortunes still didn't improve. When the financial figures for 1997 showed that Apple losses were over $1 billion (£640m), the board asked Gil to step down, and appointed Steve as CEO!

Steve and his eldest daughter, Lisa (see page 11), from an earlier relationship, taken in 1989. Steve didn't see his first child for many years, but they became close before his death.

TOP TIP

Steve was very upset when he was forced to leave Apple in 1985. But he kept an eye on his old company, and when he saw an opportunity to step in and help them, he took it!

A day in the life of Steve Jobs

What was a typical working day like for one of the world's most successful businessmen? Not surprisingly, Steve had his own way of getting the best out of himself and others.

Steve once told a reporter, 'My job is thinking, and working with people, and meeting, and email.' As the head of a fast-moving technology company, Steve often worked from the minute he got up, to the moment he went to sleep! He had a home office, and was often at his desk answering emails before the rest of the family were out of bed. He would then sit down to breakfast with his children, and share the school run with wife Laurene. After that, he would travel to the office.

Every Monday morning, Steve sat down with his top executives to discuss any big decisions that needed to be taken – for example how to fix software problems with the iPhone, or what features should be on the new iPad.

Steve's presentations were legendary. He entertained and informed audiences around the world, and added to the anticipation for new Apple products.

'Everything starts and ends with the product. We didn't sit around talking about how to drive up the stock [prices] or how to stick it to the competition. It's always about the products.'

It was Steve's job to direct what new products Apple should be creating to meet the needs of customers. Steve read industry news websites and blogs, but he also relied heavily on his own instincts. He tested every single Apple product, and never launched anything until he was 100% happy with it. Steve had no formal training as an engineer, but he had something much more valuable – the ability to put himself in the shoes of an Apple customer!

Steve always aimed to hire the most talented people. He put faith in his staff, giving them decisions to make on their own, and projects to develop. Employees also knew that at any time they might get an unexpected visit from the boss! He often dropped in unannounced to check on new developments, to keep employees motivated and on their toes!

INSPIRATION

'I'd give a lot to have Steve's taste. The way he [did] things [was] just different, and I think it [was] magical.'
Bill Gates, Microsoft founder

Steve meets Apple customers in Palo Alto, California at an iPhone launch in June 2007.

Gambling on the future

Steve had got his old job back, but there was no time to celebrate. Apple was in trouble and he needed to act quickly.

Steve never had a problem making difficult decisions if he felt they were right for the business. So when he returned to Apple, he made two very big calls. First, he reduced the company's spending – axing 70% of new products in development. As chairman he also replaced the whole board of directors who had employed him!

WOW!

By January 2000 Apple's market value had risen from $2 billion (£1.3bn) to over $16 billion (£10bn). As a reward, the Apple directors gave Steve his own Gulfstream V corporate jet!

Apple and Microsoft had been opponents for a long time. Apple was the exciting tech company that everyone loved, Microsoft the boring software developer that had a near-**monopoly** on desktop PCs' operating systems. One of Steve's first meetings was with Bill Gates, Microsoft's owner. In exchange for the right to produce and sell Microsoft Office products for the Mac, and install Microsoft's Internet Explorer web browser on all Macs sold, Gates agreed to invest $150 million (£95m) in Steve's company. Some Apple fans booed the announcement, but Steve knew that without Microsoft's support, Apple was in danger of becoming irrelevant and outdated.

Steve gives a speech at the MacWorld Expo in Tokyo. Apple products were loved worldwide.

Steve's first hit product back at Apple also proved he had a skill for giving customers what they wanted – before they knew they wanted it! In 1998 Apple unveiled the colourful iMac – a computer that looked great, and connected simply and quickly to the Internet.

It might be hard to believe today, but a multicoloured egg-shaped computer with no separate screen and no disk drive was a **revolutionary** idea. Not for the first time, Steve gambled on his instincts – and it paid off. The iMac was a huge hit, and sold for the next five years. It was also Steve's first collaboration with British designer Jonathan Ive, a man who shared Steve's love of mouth-watering product design.

HONOURS BOARD

Colours available for the new iMac

Lime
Strawberry
Blueberry
Grape
Tangerine

The iMac caught the public's imagination with its range of eye-catching colours and simple Internet connectivity.

Putting music at your fingertips

Computers had always been Apple's main business, but Steve's passion was to make products that became a part of people's daily lives. So he turned his attention to his first love – music.

Steve was a lifelong fan of the singer/songwriter Bob Dylan so he realised how strongly people felt about their favourite artists, and how much they enjoyed having music in their lives.

HONOURS BOARD
Apple's most-downloaded iTunes songs of all time*

1. *'I Gotta Feeling' by Black Eyed Peas*
2. *'Poker Face' by Lady Gaga*
3. *'Boom Boom Pow' by Black Eyed Peas*
4. *'I'm Yours' by Jason Mraz*
5. *'Viva la Vida' by Coldplay*
6. *'Just Dance' by Lady Gaga & Colby O'Donis*
7. *'Low' (feat. T-Pain) by Flo Rida*
8. *'Love Story' by Taylor Swift*
9. *'Bleeding Love' by Leona Lewis*
10. *'Tik Tok' by Ke$ha*

* February 2010

He discovered a software programme called SoundJam MP, produced by an independent software company, which allowed people to play digital MP3 files on their computer. In 2000 Apple bought the rights to it, and by January 2001, Steve announced the launch of iTunes – a simple, free download that meant Mac users could copy tracks from a CD onto their computer and play them digitally.

Steve created great products that were easy to use and amazing to look at, like the classic iPod design.

Users could also download these digital files onto portable MP3 players. There was just one drawback – although these devices had started to appear on the market, no one was buying them! In typical fashion, Steve decided it was because all the existing products didn't work properly, and looked unappealing, and set out to build something better.

With the help of hardware developer Tony Fadell and Jonathan Ive, Apple's head designer, Apple launched its first iPod on 23 October 2001, with enough storage for 1,000 songs.

The final part of the jigsaw was the iTunes Music Store, announced in April 2003, which allows users to purchase and download music online. Steve negotiated and won the cooperation of the 'big five' record companies: Sony, Warner, Universal, EMI and BMG. Apple's secure downloading process and payment system won over their concerns about the increased threat of piracy and illegal downloading.

The iTunes Store opened its doors with a library of 200,000 songs. Within a year, Apple had taken over 70% of the legal music download business, selling 85 million songs. The iTunes Music Store was named Product of the Year by *Fortune* magazine.

Music at your fingertips: a billboard in New York City spreads the word about Apple's amazing advances in music technology.

WOW!

It took Apple over three years to hit 2 billion song downloads, but it took less than 18 months to hit 2 billion app downloads!

Mission mobile

Steve had turned around Apple's fortunes, and changed the way people looked at personal computers and music. His next step? Making mobile phones exciting!

In 2001, even before Apple released its first iPod, Steve was thinking about developing a phone. He had noticed that millions of people were carrying separate music players, phones and often Blackberrys or other devices to answer their emails. He thought to himself, 'Why not combine all three in a phone?'

WOW!

Steve always drove a silver Mercedes-Benz SL55 AMG with no number plates because he took advantage of a California law that gives a maximum of six months for new vehicles to receive plates. Steve rented an identical new SL every six months.

Steve Jobs presents new Apple iPhone at the Worldwide Developers Conference in San Francisco, California, 2007.

Ever the entrepreneur, Steve invested nearly £100 million of Apple's money into developing the iPhone. He worked with programmers to write the software code, helped create the touch screen technology, and even dreamed up the phone's eye-catching look with design guru Jonathan Ive.

The iPhone went on sale on June 29, 2007 and was a massive hit. Its design, ease of use and range of functions helped sell 6 million handsets in the first year. But equally important to its success was the launch of the App Store in July 2008.

Worldwide distribution was vital to the iPhone's success. Here a woman passes an iPhone shop in China's Shandong province in 2010.

The App Store invited outside software developers to create applications, such as games, specially designed versions of Twitter, Facebook etc. – for the iPod Touch, iPhone and most recently the iPad (see pages 26-27). By allowing developers to create apps and distribute them through the App Store on iTunes, Steve gave customers thousands of reasons to buy an iPhone!

The App Store is a success story. On the day of launch, 500 apps were available but today it has grown to over half a million! In June 2010, Steve announced that there had been 5 billion app downloads in the two years since its launch, with Apple earning around $410 million (£260m) from its 30% cut of sales. Once again, Steve had gambled and won.

iPhone 3G S
100,000 个应用程序, 100,000 种惊喜体验

HONOURS BOARD

All-Time Top Paid Apps*

1. *Doodle Jump*
2. *Tap Tap Revenge 3*
3. *Pocket God*
4. *Angry Birds*
5. *Tap Tap Revenge 2.6*

All-Time Top Free Apps*

1. *Facebook*
2. *Pandora*
3. *Google Mobile App*
4. *Shazam*
5. *Movies by Flixster*

* Figures valid to January 2011

Everything that Steve touched was turning to gold, and he must have felt **invincible**. Unfortunately, a routine medical check unearthed serious health problems for the Apple boss.

Steve regularly pushed his body to the limits, working 80 or 90-hour weeks and arriving home so tired he could barely speak. In 1998, he had an operation to remove kidney stones – a painful but not life-threatening condition. But in October 2003, at a routine follow-up check, doctors discovered a **tumour** on Steve's pancreas.

HONOURS BOARD
World's most admired companies*
1. *Apple*
2. *Berkshire Hathaway*
3. *General Electric*
4. *Google*
5. *Toyota*

* Survey carried out by *Fortune* magazine, in 2008.

110 / 70

Steve's blood pressure

Steve jokes about health rumours by projecting his blood pressure onto the big screen in October 2008.

Although the condition was serious, surgeons were pleased they had caught the disease early, and also identified it as a slow-growing tumour. An operation at the time could have completely removed the cancerous growth and saved Steve's life. But he delayed the operation for a crucial nine months, choosing to treat his illness with **acupuncture**, a **vegan** diet and even by visits to a **psychic**.

Friends and family continually tried to convince Steve to change his mind, and in June 2004 he finally agreed to surgery, putting Chief Operating Officer Tim Cook in charge of Apple in his absence. Doctors operated to remove the tumour, but during the procedure they discovered that the disease had spread to his liver.

Steve and wife Laurene share a quiet moment off stage at an Apple developers' conference in San Francisco, 2011.

Steve had **chemotherapy** to shrink the cancer. After a successful but **gruelling** treatment, he spent time recovering at home in Palo Alto, California. He slowly regained strength, and returned to full-time work two years later. Steve had been softened by the experience, and though he was still a tough boss, he tried – from time to time, at least – to take the feelings of colleagues into account in his never-ending pursuit of perfection.

INSPIRATION

'Remembering that you are going to die is the best way I know to avoid the trap of thinking you have something to lose... [It's] the most important tool I've ever encountered to help me make the big choices in life.'
Steve Jobs, 2005

Reaching the End

Back at work, Steve put his energy into **revamping** Apple's personal computer division – the starting point of Apple's success. The result was another revolutionary product!

Steve knew that with a reputation for innovation he needed to keep innovating! So after the success of the iPod and the iPhone, came the iPad – a large handheld flat screen PC with a touch screen (known as a 'tablet') that offered the most popular functions that users wanted: email, gaming, music, movies and access to the Internet. It looked great, and the public fell in love with it.

An iPad displays a cover of Time *magazine featuring Steve. Many print publications now offer iPad versions for tech-hungry fans.*

The iPad was launched in April 2010, but was actually in development *before* the iPhone. Steve decided to put it on hold and launch the iPhone first, believing (correctly) that to add a phone to the iPod Touch's range of functions would be a winner with consumers.

WOW!

In January 2011, the App Store celebrated its 10 billionth download. It launched in July 2008 with 500 apps, there are now over half a million.

Environment Special: The Perils of Plastic

TIME

Inside Steve's Pad

How Jobs works
The tale of the tablet

The iPad quickly became a must-have gadget. By selling 3 million units in its first five months, it became the fastest-selling consumer electronics device in history. It not only revitalised Apple's computer sales but inspired dozens of computer manufacturers to launch their own tablet PCs, and created a whole new industry.

Unfortunately, Steve wasn't able to enjoy his success for long. In 2009 he had undergone a liver transplant. However, at the end of 2010, the cancer had returned, spreading through his body. Steve's weight dropped to just 52 kg – 20 kg less than his usual weight – and, too weak to work, he took medical leave. In August 2011, unable to return to work, Steve formally **resigned** as Apple's CEO. He died at home in October 2011, with his wife, children and sister at his bedside. He was just 56 years old.

Press around the world react to the news of Steve's death in October 2011.

INSPIRATION

'My model for business is *The Beatles*. They were four guys [who] kept each other's negative tendencies in check. They balanced each other. And the total was greater than the sum of the parts. Great things in business are never done by one person, they are done by a team of people.'
Steve Jobs, 2008

The legacy lives on

Steve worked his whole life to create products that touched people's lives. During his illness, he made plans to try and keep Apple at the top.

His story is one of the most remarkable in business history. To start a company in your parents' garage, turn it into a multimillion dollar business, get kicked out, then return and rescue it from near collapse to become one of the world's biggest companies is unique.

Steve Jobs' legacy of key Apple products – from the early Macintosh through to the iPad.

WOW!

As of October 2011, Steve is listed as inventor or co-inventor in 342 United States patents or patent applications, from computers and portable devices to speakers and keyboards. Most of these are for design!

Steve was behind every key business decision from his return to Apple in 1997 to his death in 2011. That includes the iMac, the iPod, the iPad and the iPhone. It was an amazing run of success.

He spent countless hours planning for his death, and most importantly how he could nurture an environment of creativity and innovation that would keep Apple at the top long after he was gone. Steve looked at the rise and fall of once-great technology companies like Hewlett-Packard, and how their business suffered after the original founders were no longer in charge, and was determined that wouldn't happen to Apple!

So the company invested in an executive training programme called Apple University, hiring some of the finest business professors in the United States to train future generations of Apple employees to 'think like Steve'.

The phrase is often overused, but Steve was a genius – he took incredible, imaginative, unexpected, instinctive leaps, from personal computing, to music, to phones, and always seemed to create something brilliant and totally essential. His name will be remembered forever alongside the great American **icons** Thomas Edison and Henry Ford. And his work will be remembered for generations to come.

INSPIRATION

'Steve, thank you for being a mentor and a friend. Thanks for showing what you build can change the world. I miss you.'
Mark Zuckerberg, founder of Facebook

Steve and his successor as Apple CEO, Tim Cook (right). Can Tim successfully run the company that Steve built?

Have you got what it takes to be the head of Apple?

1) Are you good with computers?
a) I can send emails and write essays. That's about it.
b) I enjoy designing birthday cards for my friends, and making videos for YouTube, but I'm no expert.
c) I love them! I've even built my own website and I'm thinking of studying programming.

2) Are you interested in new technology?
a) Are you joking? I can't even use the TV remote control.
b) Yes, but my Smart phone is smarter than me!
c) Definitely! I love finding about the next new thing – from phones to tablets to TVs.

3) Have you ever looked at something in your home, and wondered how you could improve it?
a) I've wondered how I can make mum and dad clean up after me more often!
b) I'd like a TV that can surf the Internet, but they've already invented that...
c) Of course! I'd like to be able to change TV channels with my mobile phone.

4) Do you think like an entrepreneur, and look for opportunities to make money?
a) No! Although I'm good at asking my parents for pocket money!
b) I do some babysitting on my street, but people have always asked me rather than the other way round.
c) Absolutely! I started washing neighbours' cars, now I employ three friends and we cover the whole area.

5) Are you good at managing people?
a) Nooo! I can hardly manage to get myself out of bed for school in the morning.
b) I get on well with people, but I find it hard to get my opinions across. I'd rather follow than lead.
c) Yes, I love making plans, getting everyone on board, and giving people specific tasks to do!

6) Are you prepared to take risks and keep persevering if you hit problems?
a) Probably not. If things don't go my way I usually just sulk and play Xbox.
b) I like to make a plan and stick to it. I don't know what I'd do if that plan didn't work and needed changing.
c) I sure am! Life's an adventure, and you only get out what you put in. Bring it on!

RESULTS

Mostly As: You don't sound curious or adventurous enough to take on the world. Try and think outside the box sometimes and try new experiences.

Mostly Bs: You're organised and motivated, but you need to push yourself harder, and be prepared to move outside your comfort zone to get real rewards. Be brave!

Mostly Cs: You're exactly the kind of person Steve would have loved: smart, curious, fearless and a natural leader. Work hard and one day you might change the world!

Glossary

acupuncture A system of medicine in which fine needles are inserted in the skin to treat various physical conditions.

chemotherapy The treatment of certain diseases, especially cancer, by using a mixture of drugs to 'kill' the tumour.

components Parts that go together to make a finished product (in this case a computer).

entrepreneur A person who sets up a new business, and takes on financial risks in the hope of making a profit.

extrovert An outgoing, confident person.

founder The person who starts a new company or organisation.

graphic designer Someone who uses words and pictures to create advertisements, company logos and so on.

gruelling When something is extremely tiring.

icon A person or thing that is worthy of respect or love.

incorporate To include in something.

introvert A shy, quiet person.

invincible Too powerful to be beaten.

legacy Something left or handed down to future generations.

monopoly The exclusive control of something.

mourn To feel or show sadness for someone's death.

negotiator A person who reaches a favourable agreement through discussion.

obsessed Continually thinking about something.

operating system The computer code that makes a computer work and perform tasks.

post-graduate A student who is taking a further course of study after completing a university degree.

promote To give publicity to something; raise people's awareness of something.

psychic A person who claims to have the power to see into the future.

resign To leave a job.

revamping Improving or creating a new version of something.

revitalise To breathe new life or energy into something.

revolutionary Something that involves a complete or dramatic change.

syllabus The different subject areas in a course that someone is studying.

tumour A swelling or growth on a part of the body.

vegan A person whose diet contains no meat, or other animal products like milk.

Index

INSPIRATIONAL LIVES

Contents of new titles in the series

Anthony Horowitz
978 0 7502 6808 0

A moment of inspiration
Anthony's family life
Off to Orley Farm prep school
A change for the better
Death in the family
A leap into children's writing
A day in the life of Anthony Horowitz
Anthony's big break
The Alex Rider series
TV, films and more books!
After Alex Rider
Helping charities
The impact of Anthony Horowitz
Have you got what it takes
  to be a writer?

Jay-Z
978 0 7502 6807 3

Jay-Z on top
Growing up in the projects
The wrong side of the law
A brush with death
Making history
Hitting the big time
Developing new artists
A day in the life of Jay-Z
Launching Rocawear
Selling the lifestyle
Crazy in love
Changing the game again
The impact of Jay-Z
Have you got what it takes to
  be a million dollar brand?

Amir Khan
978 0 7502 6809 7

World Champion!
A happy childhood
Bolton boy
Starting boxing
Amir the Olympian
A hero's return
Turning pro
Knocked down
Changing trainers
Success in the ring
A day in the life of Amir Khan
Charitable work
The impact of Amir Khan
Have you got what it takes
  to be a boxing champion?

Steve Jobs
978 0 7502 6806 6

Daring to be different
The orphan who found a family
The founding of Apple
Steve leaves Apple
To infinity and beyond
A change of life
A day in the life of Steve Jobs
Gambling on the future
Putting music at your fingertips
Mission mobile
Running short of time
Reaching the end
The legacy lives on
Have you got what it takes
  to be the head of Apple?

WAYLAND